100 SMALL WAYS TO

MANAGE TIME

NB

NEW BURLINGTON

A QUARTO BOOK

First published in the UK in 2017 by
New Burlington Press
The Old Brewery
6 Blundell Street
London N7 9BH

QUAR.MSWMT

ISBN: 978-0-85762-180-1

10 9 8 7 6 5 4 3 2 1

Conceived, designed,and produced by
Quarto Publishing plc
The Old Brewery
6 Blundell Street
London N7 9BH

Project editor: Kate Burkett
Senior designer: Martina Calvio
Proofreader: Caroline West
Illustrator: Rosie Scott
Art director: Caroline Guest
Creative director: Moira Clinch
Publisher: Samantha Warrington

Printed in China by 1010 Printing
International Ltd.

FOREWORD

I believe there are few basic skills more valuable
than mastering the management of our greatest
resource. So, when my editor asked me to write a
book on time management, I did not hesitate. Now,
months later, I am twice as productive as I was
before I began researching and writing this book.
Arguably, most of the 100 methods in these pages
will fail to excite you, yet I trust I have armed
you with enough silver bullets to slay the
insatiable, time-sucking monsters lurking in the
shadows hungry to gobble up your time like they
were proudly feasting on the all-you-can-eat
buffet you call life. What would you do with
another hour every day? How would you spend an
extra week every year? I urge you to remember
this sage advice: if it's important to you, you
will make the time.

Oliver Luke Delorie

WORK TIME

1

BREATHE STRESS AWAY

The instant you stop breathing, there is no longer any need to manage time (unless you believe this skill would come in handy in a future life). But no matter where you exist, stress is the enemy of effective time management. And one of the best antidotes to combat this type of stress is to relax. Take a five-minute break and some deep breaths until you feel better. Now gradually catch up.

IIII➤

The zen of time management: Breathe yourself into the present moment.

ARRIVE AND LEAVE ON TIME

Be ready to go when the light turns green and you will impress your team with your punctuality and professionalism. The more organised you are prior to any work-related gathering, the easier it will be to leave at the scheduled time (because you have been fully-present and fully-engaged). This will earn you the respect of your colleagues (who will not even notice when you get up to leave) because they are too busy dragging their feet (and drawing out the conversation).

<u>You have important work to do. Stick to the schedule.</u>

3

PLAN AHEAD

How far can you see into the future? Even
if you can only glimpse tomorrow, plan
ahead. What needs to get done? What would
you like to get done? Spontaneity has
its place, though if you know what you're
doing, when and how (in advance) you will
be more effective when the rubber meets the
road and it's time to step on
the accelerator.

Fail to plan and
you plan to fail.

DON'T WAIT FOR LATECOMERS

Locking the door when the meeting starts is effective, but perhaps a little too harsh for the more sensitive members of your team (especially if they are the ones running late). A better approach is to begin without them. Minutes add up (just ask my former accountant, who arranges her life — and bills her clients — in six-minute increments). You are only as strong as the weakest link in your team, but you don't have to let these tardy individuals hinder your progress.

Whose time is more important?

TELECONFERENCING

Why spend hours in traffic, queuing,
going through security or having to
slow down for every speed bump on the
road to your next meeting? Technology
has made it possible to join your
colleagues virtually anywhere in
the world they wish to meet. Both
hardware and software teleconferencing
solutions are affordable, easy to use
and ultimately help you conserve your
most precious resource: time.

Your simulated presence is
sufficient for most meetings.

6

RECRUIT YOUR FRIENDS

How much time and money do you or your company spend on recruiting talent and muscle? Where do you even begin to look? Do you hire third-party contractors to rustle up executive, creative, technical and physical muscle for you? If you feel confident vouching for new hires from your social circle(s), you can stop paying headhunters the bounty they may or may not deserve.

 You are a built-in reference for your friends, which speeds up the hiring process.

7

TEMPLATES ARE TIME SAVERS

No need to reinvent the wheel. There are thousands of templates available for everything, from budgeting to 3D printing. Get acquainted with copy and paste, because thousands have gone before you and done half the work. Stand on the shoulders of giants by utilising templates to increase your productivity so you can get more done in less time.

Utilise templates to increase your productivity at work and at home so you can get more done in less time.

THE EIGHTY TWENTY RULE

Traditionally referred to as The Pareto Principle, this mathematical formula was first recognised by an Italian economist in 1906 and suggests that 80% of your results come from 20% of your efforts, while 80% of your effort produces only 20% of your results. To get the most bang for your buck from now on, take some time to ponder how applying this principle to your personal and professional endeavours could be a game-changer.

Get more of what you want and less of what you don't.

9 FOCUS ON RESULTS vs ACTIVITIES

How much time do you spend being 'busy'?
Just because you are engaged in blog-able
activities doesn't necessarily mean you are
being productive or using your time wisely.
Remember how delegating and leveraging your
time can create enormous rewards? In the same
way, emphasising 'deliverables' and 'project
outcomes' (as opposed to being immersed in
and preoccupied by daily duties and routines)
will help to concentrate your energies so
you achieve tangible results — so much so
that you may pleasantly surprise yourself
(and your boss).

Finally, results
translate into perks
and benefits quicker
than just spinning
your wheels on the
treadmill. What do
you want out of life?

When managing
your time, focus
on quality
vs quantity.

TAKE CALCULATED RISKS

If you have ever created a P&L Statement, conducted a SWOT analysis (which stands for Strengths, Weaknesses, Opportunities and Threats) or simply doodled a Pros and Cons list on a napkin, you were on the right track. Gathering as much information as you can before making a decision is smart, though give yourself parameters (and a certain amount of time) to assess the risks, because as much as trying something new will excite you, it may also be frightening, so mitigate any potential loss by knowing what you're up against.

Be careful to avoid the time-trap of 'analysis paralysis'.

11

PRIORITISE

When responsibilities pile up,
it's not the end of the world,
because you already prioritise
based on your likes and dislikes.
If something is important,
you will find the time. But
what happens when there is too
much on your plate and you get
overwhelmed? You do what the
professionals do: complete one
thing at a time. Not sure what to
do first? Just think: what needs
doing first?

You can't go wrong
by greasing the
squeakiest wheel.

12 CONSOLIDATE

The more discombobulated your life, the more time you will waste (and can never recapture). If an ocean of commitments, debt or chores is flooding your boat and you feel like you're sinking, it's time to bail yourself out by focusing on the biggest leak in your ship. If the rope is starting to unravel, you are at the mercy of the tide. Mergers will solidify your position and provide a sense of security and permanence.

Herd the cats so you can relax.

13

IDENTIFY THREE OUTCOMES

There are more than three possible outcomes to
many situations, but for now, let's keep it
simple and pinpoint three. Imagine what would
happen if someone did the opposite of what
you expected them to do. What if a project
turned out better than expected? What could
happen if things fell apart completely? Would
you be able to handle it/fix it/let it go? And
what if the worst comes to pass? Focusing your
attention only on potential negative outcomes
is counterproductive, so keep the balance
with two positive outcomes and one less-than-
perfect scenario.

 Manage your resources
better by predicting
possible future outcomes.

14 SINGLE TASK

People boast about how great they are at multitasking, but according to experts, it's not something to be proud of. Regardless of what your cousin accomplishes in less time than anyone she knows, the people-in-the-know say we are not wired for multitasking. Yes, things are getting done, but at what level? If you are distracted, you are not fully concentrating.

What does work, on the other hand, is the philosophy and practise of 'single-tasking' which means focusing your attention and resources on one person/place/thing at a time, so you can really get a sense of what's going on and thus achieve better results.

If a project or hobby or other pursuit is meaningful to you, why not give it your full attention... even just for 30 minutes a day?

 Focus on one thing at a time.

LEARN TO DELEGATE

What if you could clone yourself? Would you do things differently? What would you focus on? Use your time wisely by learning to delegate repetitive tasks or activities you don't particularly enjoy. You are not an expert in every subject or project (nor do you take pleasure in performing every task), but others are. Your burden is someone else's passion, so recruit other people to do the heavy lifting (so you can focus on what you do best).

Get other people to do your
dirty work for you.

16

LEVERAGE TECHNOLOGY

Every day, new technologies are
being thought of, programmed and
manufactured into existence to make
your life better, easier, more
convenient, more enjoyable; and to
give you more information, advantages,
a longer life and more time, love
and resources. Tall order. Embrace
practical advances in science and
technology that promise to serve you
and you will grow and benefit in ways
you could never have imagined.

You ain't seen nothing yet.
And, relatively speaking,
this is only the beginning.

17 GO PAPERLESS

Paper and paper products may always be a part of our lives, but you can save time by reducing the amount you use and waste by buying less (or none at all), by digitising your documents and by requesting that others you do business with do the same when dealing and communicating with you. Set an example in your workplace or at home and keep things simple.

Reducing the amount of paper you use will reduce clutter on your desk and in your filing cabinets (which you could eventually get rid of). As you know, creating and coping with clutter takes up time. Luckily, there are apps aplenty that will minimise your dependence on paper, while maximising your enjoyment of your business and personal pursuits.

Save time and trees.
Go paperless.

USE THE RIGHT TOOL FOR THE JOB

A plumber comes to your house to fix a leaky tap. She is finished in five minutes and charges you £100. Thinking to yourself, it's time for a career change, you ask the plumber why she is so expensive. With a smile, she says '£10 for the part; £90 for knowing what the problem was, what tool to use and how to use it.' Renting or borrowing the tools you need will save you time because you don't have to move, store, insure, clean, repair and eventually replace them.

You wouldn't use a kitchen fork to weed your garden.

19 MAKE A TO-DO LIST ON A POST-IT NOTE

The less you have to do, the less you will be plagued by tension headaches. Nothing too-monumental can fit on a Post-It note, nor can an insurmountable list of things-needing-doing. Portable and sticky, there is less chance of you losing a little note like this, so keep it close and it will repay you by keeping you focused on your mission, should you choose to accept it.

Bright and sticky, these little square pieces of paper revolutionised productivity.

STUDY BEST PRACTICES

What is the best way to solve the problem? What are your most successful peers, the competition you are most envious of or your wisest family members doing to solve a similar issue? How do the pros crack the code you are stumbling to decipher? The information you need is out there. You just have to find it, understand it and implement it. And if at first you don't succeed, try and try again.

Seek out, study and implement the most effective policies and procedures you can find.

21

CREATE SYSTEMS

As much as spontaneously making-it-up-as-
you-go along can be exhilarating, the best
families, organisations and businesses
function at their peak when systems have
been put in place to structure, automate and
ensure an agreed-upon level of performance.
The better the system, the better the outcome.
Look to your colleagues, industry and your
competition to identify where and how to
employ systems in your public or private
framework, so you may leverage your time and
resources to consistently produce higher
quality goods and services (or complete
household chores and enjoy more family time).

Systems are the secret
formula to success in
any human effort.

STOP PROCRASTINATING

There are 24 hours in a day and maintaining your life by sleeping, eating, etc. only consumes on average 10-12 hours (maximum) per each 24-hour stretch. Have you ever considered what you could possibly accomplish by just getting off your butt and doing whatever you daydream about? Talk yourself into action with some rich reward (or punishment, if that's your thing), because only you can motivate you. Schedule your time, do what needs to be done and you will surprise yourself.

What are you waiting for?

23

ANALYSIS PARALYSIS

Try not to fall prey to the futile
beast of 'analysis paralysis', wherein
you succumb to the temptations of
information overload, and in the process
waste a lot of time, ending up only
going in circles and not taking any
definite action (or making a decision).
It's easy to get clobbered with facts,
figures, statistics and data, but no one
has all the answers at the right time
(nor does anyone expect you to sagely
peer into the future like a seer). As
long as you remain flexible, you can
always correct your course as you
move forward.

Make the best decision
with the information
you have available.

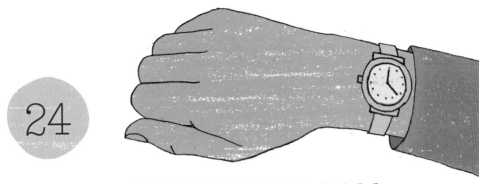

GIVE YOURSELF DEADLINES

You summon an enormous amount of energy,
creativity and adrenaline when you cram to
complete your project or meet a deadline.
Setting realistic deadlines for yourself
will help keep you motivated and organised
so that you can wrap up your work in a
timely manner. If meeting your deadlines
hasn't come easily in the past, don't fret.
The more you challenge yourself to fulfill
your self-imposed obligations (and do so),
the sooner you will reap the rewards given
to those who have gotten the hang of it.

Do what you say you will
do, on time, and you will
transform your life.

SURROUND YOURSELF WITH PRODUCTIVE PEOPLE

How well does your best friend manage his/her time? And who do you frequently call, text or email for advice? How organised, productive and satisfied with their lives are they? Average the organisational capacity, financial literacy and lifestyle choices of the five people you spend the most time with and you will have an accurate picture of who you are (including how adept you are when it comes to time-mastery). If birds of a feather flock together, are the birds in your nest prolific and productive or late and lazy?

You can learn good habits by osmosis.

MAKE YOUR BREAKS PRODUCTIVE

How do you spend your coffee or cigarette breaks? Do you drown them with coffee or watch them go up in a puff of smoke? Why not respond to important texts and emails, return phone calls, engage in meaningful conversation with a peer, find somewhere quiet to meditate, stretch, read or plan the rest of your day? Every minute counts.

15 minutes per break x 500 breaks per working year = 125 hours.

LEAVE WORK AT WORK

Like fans from two opposing football
clubs, work and play are best kept
separate from each other. Unless
you are working 80 hours a week for
yourself (so you don't have to work 40
hours a week for someone else), when
it's time to turn off your computer,
set the alarm, sweep the floor or
lock the door, it's then time to give
your full attention to the people
and activities you love. This means
disengaging from work so you can be
completely present when you get home,
down to the pub for happy hour or to
the cabin on the lake.

Don't let work come between
you and what matters most.

28 CREATE A FILING SYSTEM

Do you like to bake? Creating a filing system can be as easy-as-pie or a piece-of-cake (depending on which you prefer). Keeping your important documents organised (let alone in one place) will shave days of time off your life which were formerly spent searching for misplaced bills, receipts, contracts (and the recipe for your favourite comfort food) if you have a filing system in place. But there's no need to complicate matters; keep your archival process simple and, regardless of which way the wind blows, you can expect smooth sailing from now on.

P.S. It's okay to ask for help if you need it.

Set it and
forget it.

29

KEEP AN IDEA FILE

What a great idea! When was the last time you woke up in the middle of the night and swore to yourself you would remember 'the secret of the universe' bequeathed to you in your dreams, only to wake up hours later desperately wracking your brain for the answer to all things?

Once you have an idea file, everything you jot down in the notebook beside your bed will end up in one place, organised and alphabetised. This idea file will become a gold mine that you can visit whenever you need inspiration.

 The point of keeping an idea file is to keep your ideas organised, and all in one place, so you don't have to scramble to find (or remember) them.

 # LEVERAGE YOUR TIME

How is your time best spent? When are you 'in the zone'? Taking advantage of the moments and activities that produce the most favourable results is the most productive use of your time. Are you good with a sling-shot? How can you kill two (or three) birds with one stone? Do you want to learn a new language? Master it while working out or sitting in traffic. Want to catch up on emails on the bus? This trumps the entertaining (but useless) pastime of people-watching. Leveraging your time is not multitasking; leverage means spending your time on what gives you the most results (see The Eighty Twenty Rule on page 16).

When time stands still, keep moving.

TOUCH THINGS ONCE

When something comes across your desk,
don't pick it up or look at it unless
you are going to file it immediately
or respond to the request. If you open
an email, read it and reply to it right
away. Don't touch anything more than
once. If you are cleaning out your
garage, everything you unearth should be
dealt with then-and-there. There is no
point moving something more than once,
nor spending an inordinate amount of time
deciding what to do with said object a
second (or third) time.

Deal with it and
be done with it.

32

AVOID MEETINGS WITH NO AGENDA

Meetings without an agenda are parties. If there is work to be done and/or decisions to be made, meetings without an agenda are pointless and a huge waste of time, unless they are brainstorming sessions (in which case, 'brainstorming session' should be on the To-Do list). You know what meetings are like at your workplace. Does business get done? Is attendance mandatory? If not, minimise the amount of time you squander at such functions and keep your nose to the grindstone instead.

Every minute you spend on something is a minute you cannot spend on something else.

ME TIME

33 ESTABLISH ROUTINES

If you are reading this book, there is a good chance that you are prone to the willy-nilly style of time management and tend to fly-by-the-seat-of-your-pants. But, like most people, you can establish basic routines around your morning, afternoon or evening rituals, based on what you tend to do at the same time each day. Maintaining and supplementing your existing routines can be as simple as acknowledging the structure already in place and adapting new habits or activities into the mix.

Learn to act like a robot and they may spare you if they ever take over.

34

NO THANKS

Acknowledging (then graciously declining) any offers to do something you don't really want to do will free up an enormous amount of time, money and energy. Trying to please everyone doesn't work (but you probably know that already). Saying 'Thanks, but no thanks' takes courage and practice, but it's possible to stand up for yourself and declutter your timeline. Here are some scenarios to give you an idea of how easy it can be.

The benefits of saying 'Thanks, but no thanks' will reduce headaches, stress, time and money. Trying to please everyone doesn't work.

THEM: 'Mom, can you wash, fold, and iron my shirt for work?'

YOU: 'Oh honey, I'm flattered that you appreciate how skilled I am at doing your washing, but I think it's time you learned how to do it yourself. Here, let me show you how.'

THEM: 'Can I borrow some money?'

YOU: 'Thank you for asking, but I'm (we're) on a budget.'

THEM: 'We were thinking we could spend Christmas with you.'

YOU: 'That sounds lovely, but we've booked a trip to [insert some place far away].'

THEM: 'Will you go out with me?'

YOU: 'Oh, I'm flattered that you asked, but I'm already seeing someone.'

THEM: 'Let's have lunch (read: gossip and complain about our coworkers) today.'

YOU: 'Thanks, but I packed my lunch. Maybe another time.'

35

NIP PROBLEMS
IN THE BUD

Like Jimi Hendrix, chop down those
mountains with the length of your
hand while they are still mole hills.
The longer you let things fester
and germinate, the more they grow
(sometimes out of control). Better
to say what needs to be said, or do
what needs to be done, before things
get blown out of proportion. Melting
snowflakes before they become snowballs
will save you more than time; how
about fewer headaches, less stress,
and reduced aggravation? Extinguish
the spark before it becomes
an inferno.

An ounce of prevention is
worth a pound of cure.

36

IMPROVE YOUR DECISION MAKING PROCESS

How do you currently make decisions? Carve out some creative time to identify what is important to you. Then train your gut or intuition or ouija board or astrologer or mother-in-law to help you devise a process for making better decisions faster. The less time you spend mulling over which way to go, the more time you will have to explore the side roads where all the treasure lies hidden and waiting.

When you get to the fork in the road, take it.

37

WORK WITH YOUR NATURAL CYCLES

Are you a morning person or a night owl? If you have yet to give your natural rhythms any thought, start to notice when you are the most creative, productive and energetic. Most people are most productive when they are least tired, though studies show that others are at their creative best just before bed. If you happen to tend to your garden based on the cycles of the moon, acknowledging your own daily and monthly cycles (known as bio-rhythms) is not too much of a stretch. But not everyone dances to the beat of the natural world, so another approach to making the most of your time is to know when you ebb and when you flow.

Attempt the most difficult tasks when you have the most energy.

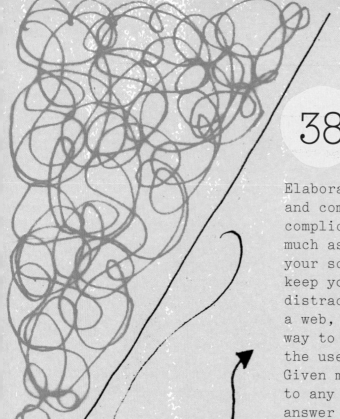

38 SIMPLIFY YOUR LIFE

Elaborate, sophisticated and complex, life will complicate your life as much as you let it. Filling your schedule just to keep yourself busy (read: distracted) tangles you in a web, from which the only way to escape is to opt for the user-friendly version. Given multiple alternatives to any problem, the simplest answer is often the best, because simplicity moves heaven and earth. Free up some extra time and escape before the spider gets you.

Vanilla is the most popular flavour of ice cream.

MINDFULNESS MATTERS

Wisdom comes with experience, yet mindfulness can be had at any point on your journey. Don't feel like you have to buy a one-way ticket to India, climb a mountain in search of a guru, don a loin cloth and sit in a cave with your eyes closed chanting OM until you reach enlightenment. All you need to perceive life with more awareness is to metaphorically contemplate the fruits of your labour (time) as they appear on the tree.

Time appears to disappear in a state of mindfulness.

40
KNOW YOUR LIMITS

Who or what takes up too much of your time? Even if you do not currently practise setting or honouring limits on the demands for your time, everyone has their tipping point. You may be extremely generous, but later feel depleted and burned out. By intentionally placing limits on your responsibilities, you free up time for who and what matters most.

One provincial lottery corporation's motto is 'Know your limit. Play within it.'

SCHEDULE HOUSEHOLD CHORES

You may have grown up with a calendar on the refrigerator scheduling everyone's household chores. And if your parents didn't impose this strict regime on you, perhaps your well-meaning roommates in college requested that you pitch in. Nonetheless, scheduling (and delegating) household chores will help ensure the house is kept clean and tidy. And done so in a timely manner. Remember to ask for everyone's feedback as to the time commitment required for each chore, so the list can evolve as everyone grows.

A minute saved on the dishes is a minute earned in the garden.

SETTING BOUNDARIES

Extending yourself beyond your limits to satisfy what you believe other people need will often leave you feeling depleted, emotionally and physically (and sometimes spiritually). The reverse is true too. By not guarding yourself against undue requests on your time, you compromise control over your life and weaken your position even further. Setting (and maintaining) boundaries is a sign of healthy relationships, both at home and at work. As long as you communicate what you need, when and why, you can't go wrong.

When setting boundaries, begin by saying 'I feel...' and 'I need...'

43

ONE MINUTE SAVES FIVE

Research shows that
every minute spent
planning saves five
minutes of execution.
Can you imagine being five
times more effective? What
would you do with all the
extra time? Of course, the
more strategic your planning,
the better your results,
but practice makes perfect.
Heck, with this tactic at your
fingertips, you have everything
you need to take control of your
life. Now take five minutes and
let it all soak in.

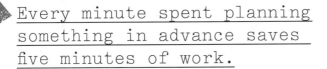

<u>Every minute spent planning
something in advance saves
five minutes of work.</u>

44

DON'T SPEND TWENTY MINUTES ON A FIVE-MINUTE PROBLEM

Self-explanatory, this small yet worthwhile strategy to manage your time will flip a switch in your mind (if you didn't just have a Eureka moment as you read the title). It seems like common sense, but how do you judge what deserves five minutes of your problem-solving prowess, and what requires 20? That depends on the problem.

Beyond obvious, this tactic will make you a master of time itself.

5-Minute Problem: What to make for dinner?
20+ Minute Solution: Sit down with a pile of cookbooks and drool over every photo.
5-Minute Solution: Open the fridge, pick three ingredients and get cooking.

5-Minute Problem: What to wear on a date?
20+ Minute Solution: Spend the day on the high street and buy a new wardrobe on credit.
5-Minute Solution: Open the wardrobe, select your three favourite outfits, try them on and decide based on what makes you feel the sexiest.

5-Minute Problem: What correspondence to respond to?
20+ Minute Solution: Procrastinate for a while, then spend hours replying to everyone.
5-Minute Solution: Identify the messages requiring your immediate attention, respond to these and delegate/ignore the rest.

5-Minute Problem: What movie to watch?
20+ Minute Solution: Go online and fall into the vortex of viewing trailer after trailer.
5-Minute Solution: Scroll the selections with your eyes closed and randomly pick one.

5-Minute Problem: What brand of product to buy?
20+ Minute Solution: Get bogged down in the details of consumer watchdog reports.
5-Minute Solution: Follow your instincts and choose the best product based on your needs and preferences.

45 BRAINSTORM

Rule number one. There is no seat at the creative brainstorming table for the left-brain, analytical editor. Set aside an allotted amount of time to scheme, concoct and invent new ways to manage what needs to be managed.

Rule number two. There are no rules. The benefit to what some call a brain-dump is to capture as many pie-in-the-sky ideas that you can (without judgement). Yes, some brainchildren will come out hair-brained, but some could very well lead to enormous breakthroughs in every aspect of your life. If this isn't a good use of your time, what is?

Investing in a brainstorming session will yield astronomical returns.

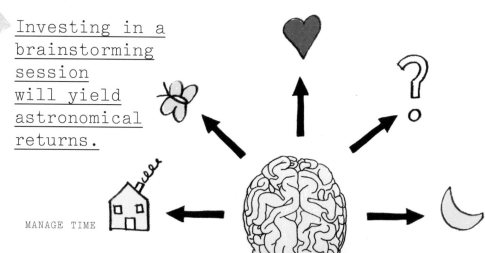

46

WAKE UP EARLIER

Feel like there aren't enough hours in the day? Even though your alarm clock may be your sworn enemy, going to bed (and getting up) with the sun (depending on where you live) may be all you need to get more done. Want more peace and quiet? There are fewer barking dogs, unhappy children and lawnmowers making a racket at 6am (not to mention less traffic on the way to work).

The early bird gets the worm.

TAKE CARE OF YOURSELF

Managing your time requires at least one thing: you. If you are not ship-shape, getting anything done takes twice as long (if not more). As you know, maintaining good emotional, physical and spiritual health is essential to survival (let alone thriving in any venture). Unfortunately, no one knows what you need quite like you do, but that means you are solely responsible for your health, wealth and happiness.

Grass doesn't strain to grow.
And neither should you.

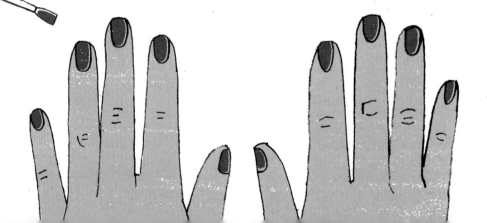

Read a self-improvement book: No matter how you desire to change your life, there are countless advisors (both accredited and otherwise) eager to share their tips and tricks on how to improve your circumstances. Visit a library or bookstore and take your pick.

Exercise: Up down, up down; one, two, three, four. If it don't hurt, it won't work. Gain is painful. But if it were easy, it wouldn't be worth it. Put on your running shoes and walk around the block. If you make it out alive, put a spring in your step and jog next time.

Stay in bed on purpose: Brush your teeth, go to the loo and grab a bowl of cereal. Now get back into bed. And stay there. Yes, you will most likely feel guilty (and maybe even anxious), but take a deep breath and enjoy it. Turn off your phone and go back to sleep.

Grow your own vegetables: By hook or by crook, eek out a garden plot and ask your neighbour with the Autumn Fair-winning acorn squash how to grow your own... veggies. Come harvest time, you may just find yourself in ecstasy (the legal kind).

Take a mental health day: Book yourself an appointment at the local spa and pamper yourself with pleasure. Get a massage, facial, manicure and pedicure and soak in a bubble bath (or hot pool) before you munch on sprouts and sip wheatgrass juice for lunch.

COMBINE ERRANDS

Do you have time to stop at the supermarket on the way to swimming lessons? And do you need petrol? Get it on the way back. Most people naturally have a typical inclination and customary wherewithal to incorporate as many tasks as they can into their existing schedules. If this is news to you, don't feel bad. But from now on, see how many flowers you can pollinate in one day.

Watch two birds with one set of binoculars.

ROCKS, PEBBLES, SAND

Do you struggle to find
time for what matters most?
With the Rock-Pebble-Sand
approach to prioritising,
consider your time as a
jar you must fill with
your list of tasks. Rocks
are high-priority, like
filling your near-empty
petrol tank. Pebbles are not
urgent, but important, such
as decluttering your desk
or email inbox. Finally,
you fill the rest of your
jar up with sand, the low-
priority activities, like
binge-watching television
shows. But if you fill up
your jar with cat videos
(sand), where will you put
the pebbles and rocks?

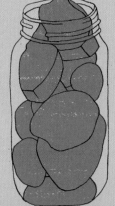

Fill your jar with the
big (most important)
rocks first.

YOUR PREFERRED COMMUNICATION METHOD

50

If there are billions of ways to do everything, there are perhaps as many ways to communicate with other people. Knowing this, you are bound to misinterpret both the obvious and more subtle spoken and unspoken messages in your daily communications, not to mention be misunderstood yourself. This is why it is crucial to let others know how you like to receive information. Do you prefer face-to-face, text messages, an email or a phone call? Get on the same page, so you can be reading the same book, at the same speed, at the same time.

As the song goes: The more we get together, the happier we'll be.

51

PUT PERSONAL ITEMS WHERE YOU CAN FIND THEM

When you get home, put your purse, keys, wallet and phone in the same place. And when you get in your car, do the same. A friend of mine regularly fields calls from friendly strangers and the local authorities informing him of the recovery of his lost personal items. No doubt, he is often stressed about the situation, but who wouldn't be? You don't need any more stress or delays in your life. So do as I say, not as my friend does...

Repetition is the mother of time management.

MAXIMISE DRIVE TIME

How much time do you spend driving to
and from work or school and attending
social and sporting activities? What
would make waiting in traffic more
productive for you? Instead of getting
agitated, could you make a point of
relaxing by doing some deep breathing
exercises or listening to an inspiring
or entertaining audio book or podcast?
Or make some important hands-free
phone calls? When was the last time
you called your mother?

Consider drive time
as free time.

PAY ALL YOUR BILLS ONLINE AT THE SAME TIME

Like debt consolidation, paying the piper all at once will not only save you time, but also all-but-eliminate the nagging feeling that comes when you have overlooked the details. Outstanding bills due at varying times and requiring different payment methods will only haunt you when all you want to do is sleep (as if you didn't have enough to think about before bed). Online banking, instant transfers and subscription services make paying your bills online at the same time a breeze, so there is no excuse not to be doing it.

Set up recurring, automatic bill payments and be done with it.

START SMALL

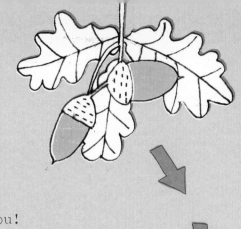

You were once a speck of
protoplasm. And now look at you!
Everyone and everything has its roots
in formless energy, which proves
that no matter how small your humble
beginnings, you can and will grow.
Mindfully engineer your life according
to what you value most, challenging
yourself when appropriate. When
starting something new, be patient,
for nature has its own timeline.

Take one step at a
time, because Rome
wasn't built in a
day. Nor is anything
of any significance.

55

KEEP A CLOCK ON THE WALL

Tick-tick-tocking goes the clock, its only purpose to remind you of your mastery of time (or lack thereof). Regardless of your positive or adversarial relationship to the precise tally of your life experience, tracking your second-by-second or minute-to-minute association to how you spend your existence is crucial when it comes to planning and organising your day. Again, what you can measure and track, you can control.

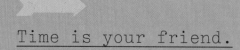

Time is your friend.

56

HIRE A VIRTUAL ASSISTANT

Although virtual assistants have changed the way we work, it remains to be seen if/when/how they may change the way we play. But if you are self-employed, then 'me' time is often 'go' time, in which case hiring someone to do the repetitive, time-consuming or mind-numbing tasks can save your life from the clutches of the endless abyss where free time doesn't exist. Overseas help is more affordable, though no matter where you outsource your assistance, be sure to ask for (and verify) references before you shell out your hard earned shekels.

Experience shows that you get what you pay for.

57

THE EASY RULE OF LIFE

According to my mentor, if you do what's easy and comfortable, your life will end up difficult and uncomfortable, whereas if you do the difficult and uncomfortable, life will be easy and comfortable. In other words, there is a price to pay if you wish to achieve a desired result. At first, managing your time may be difficult and uncomfortable, but it will pay dividends for the rest of your life.

If you want something you have never had, you have to do something you have never done.

58 COORDINATE YOUR FAMILY SCHEDULES

Having a family dinner and synchronising your watches instead of enjoying a decadent dessert is extreme, but you get the idea. You likely already communicate enough to cooperate, but you can always sand the edges to a smooth finish. And even if it never seems to work, when it does work, it will feel like planned perfection. The point is to build a well-oiled machine so you can enjoy more 'me' time.

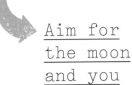

Aim for the moon and you will hit the stars.

59

DON'T MAKE DECISIONS

If you feel you are metaphorically sinking in quick sand, paralysed by 'analysis paralysis' and wasting time worried about making the 'wrong' decision, first things first: There is no such thing as a 'wrong' decision. If you find you are headed down an uninspiring path, it's quite alright to stop, course-correct and give yourself permission not to make a decision. This is a temporary bluff, but an effective poker hand when played at the right time.

Decide not to decide.

60

SCHEDULE HOBBIES

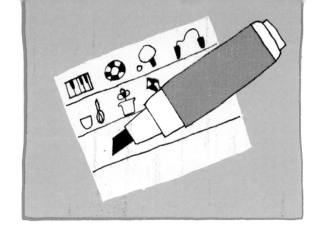

Instead of pencilling-in playtime on your calendar, use a big, black felt-tip pen! Without a strong commitment to spending time doing things that inspire and relax you, a healthy work-life balance will elude you. And, as long as your life is out of balance, you may never grasp the concept of (nor practise) effective time management. Don't worry if you can only squeeze in an hour a week; just do it. Like saving 10% of everything you earn, the compounding interest will accumulate and pay off big-time in the future.

If you can't find the time to enjoy (or explore) a hobby, it's time for a check-up from the neck up.

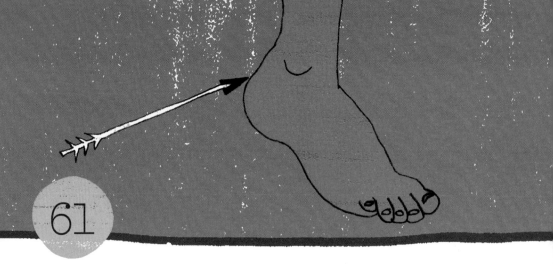

DON'T START PROJECTS OFF ON THE BACK FOOT

Belief is the best guarantee, but if you are not fully committed to doing whatever it takes to successfully complete a project, do not begin it in the first place. Talk about a waste of time. This figurative Achilles Heel is the bane of countless entrepreneurs, creative people and adventurous types; so much so that volumes could be written on this basic philosophy alone. If you cannot see the end in perfectly clear detail, do not take another step. Yes, failure is best seen as a learning opportunity, but why learn the hard way?

 Follow your heart, but only if it's in the right place.

SCREEN YOUR CALLS

Regardless of what or who you believe
is responsible for creating everything,
voicemail is divine. Reducing the time
you spend on unproductive details like
dealing with phone calls from every end
of the earth on every imaginable subject
is akin to breaching the vaults of heaven
itself. Secretary, personal assistant or
family member, they deserve credit for
saving years of your time you may otherwise
spend wading through the weeds of the swamp
otherwise known as your voicemail inbox.
Barricade your precious time.

Brad Pitt's trail-blazing
character in *Fight Club* says
'I never pick up my phone.'

63 PUT TIME LIMITS ON ACTIVITIES

If you know that washing your hair takes an hour from start to finish, set a timer. Yes, this takes the fun out of it, so instead put a time limit on tasks you don't particularly enjoy. Only spend one hour a day doing the washing. Or limit Christmas shopping to one trip, one day or one week (unless this is the highlight of your year, in which case you may forget time management altogether). But if this is a chore, do whatever you can to accommodate everyone's wish list into your itinerary. And if you don't succeed, don't try and try again; just blame Santa.

You rarely work past the end of your shift, so why not hold yourself accountable to little ol' you at other times?

64

IGNORE MISSED CALLS

You have better things to do than
to chase down a missed call. Often
the person won't even pick up, which
means you waste even more time
leaving them a message. Phone tag
is a vicious cycle; not a game you
want to get caught up playing. If
someone doesn't leave a message, it
wasn't important. So why should it be
important to you?

Leave a message
at the beep.

KEEP A TIME DIARY

Keep a diary or log book of your routine and extra-curricular activities and you will see what tasks are swallowing the most time in one gulp. Many self-employed and/or creative people want to know how many hours to bill a client, or how long it takes to complete a painting, sculpture or sound recording. What you measure, you can track. And what you can track, you can control. Are you on top of your day or not?

Put your priorities
in perspective.

66

FORGET TIME ALTOGETHER

Forgetting about time management altogether is perhaps counter-intuitive in a book about time management, but if being at the helm and overseeing all things in your personal and professional life is stressing you out and causing harm in one form or another, take a break from it all. When was the last time you weren't responsible for managing, facilitating, controlling or engineering whatever was happening? If time flies when you're having fun, does time slow to a standstill to watch you suffer when things aren't so grand?

Is time your friend or your enemy? Either way, you get to choose.

GOOD TIME

DATE NIGHT

One isn't the loneliest number. Implement a date night to spend one-on-one time with a special person. It could be a mother—son, friend—friend, or husband—wife date. Everyone likes to feel special, including your dog. A dog date might mean taking your pooch for an extra-long walk.

Spending quality time with just one person enables you to concentrate, listen and talk to them in a focused way — which makes them feel special. In return, they will do the same for you and you will feel valued, understood and connected.

What better way to spend your valuable time than this?

Spend quality time with the important people in your life.

BLOCK OUT DISTRACTIONS

What diverts your attention and disturbs your zen-like concentration when you're in the zone? In any case, text message alerts, blinking advertisements, persistent children, frequent emails, coworkers buzzing around your office like bees in search of honey and myriad other distractions will knock you off balance if you're not careful, leaving you reeling from the interference so much that it may be hard to regain composure. But you must recover.

You can't do the big things if you're distracted by the little things.

69

DOES IT MATTER

Nihilists would disagree, but if it matters to you, that is enough to keep going. If you are ever doubtful whether something is worth your time and attention, ask yourself this question. You may just reveal an inner truth or opposing viewpoint that could help you clarify the issue. Ultimately, everything you do and decide and devote your time and energy to is up to you. This is why questioning everything can shed a light on your motivations and inspiration in the first place.

Time has a way of showing you what matters.

70 IGNORE RIGHT - MOOD PROCRASTINATION

If you suffer from a common ailment known as right-mood procrastination, and depending on where you live, your moods change more than the weather (which is why waiting for the 'right' time to do anything is a recipe for an unfulfilling and dissatisfying life), you may fail and experience setbacks. However, failure is only proof that something doesn't work, and setbacks alert you to the fact there is another way to realise a goal; you just have to figure it out.

Adopt the attitude that you will learn as you go.

Thought: 'I don't have the right education.'
Action: With enough belief in yourself, you will enroll in a course and learn from those that have gone before you.

Thought: 'I'm waiting until I have enough [insert resource].'
Action: Do what you can with what you have. When you encounter an obstacle (real or imagined) summon your own tangible and intangible reserves of support.

Thought: 'My astrologer said it's not the right time.'
Action: If you find value in spiritual counselling, get the information you need to know when to step on the accelerator, so when the light turns green you can finally move forward.

Thought: 'I don't feel like it.'
Action: What don't you feel like? Savouring the victory of accomplishing your goals and realising your dreams? Sit down at the computer, go out to the workshop, pick up the phone or open that drawer. The minute you give your attention to something, invisible forces will come to your aid.

Thought: 'I'm scared I may fail.'
Action: If you let fear make your decisions, you will always be miserable. Motivational speakers recommend feeling the fear and doing it anyway. What have you go to lose?

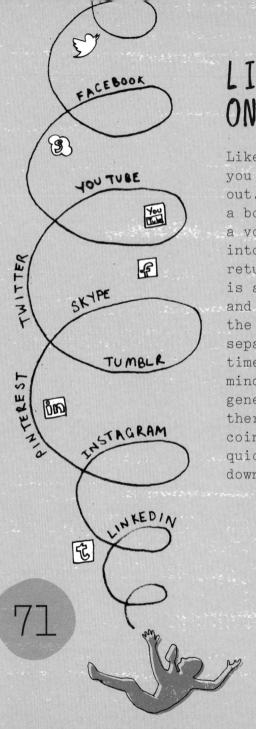

FACEBOOK

YOU TUBE

TWITTER

SKYPE

TUMBLR

PINTEREST

INSTAGRAM

LINKEDIN

71

LIMIT TIME SPENT ON SOCIAL MEDIA

Like a well, if you fall in, you may never find your way out. Social media websites are a bottomless pit. And, like a vortex, you may get sucked into the vastness, never to return. Internet connectivity is a boon to relationships, and has been known to bridge the gaps between people separated by distance and time, while fostering like-minded connections that span generations and interests. But there are two sides to every coin and time can (and does) quickly evaporate when you go down the rabbit hole...

Being famous on social media is like being rich in Monopoly.

FIND TIME TO PLAY

For all you know, amusing yourself with
various diversions and entertaining your
inner child with creative capers will
free your spirit and encourage a natural
flow to time management. You will no
longer worry about fitting everything
into your schedule, nor encapsulating the
essence of any activity without seeing
it as fluid and capable of breaching
the boundaries of your own (and others')
expectations of what it should be.

'Play is the highest
form of research.'
~ Albert Einstein.

73

EXPECT DELAYS

It is inevitable that you will encounter setbacks, delays, frustrations and obstacles to whatever you endeavour to accomplish. Nature has a timeline it sticks to, like clockwork. Sometimes you are travelling at the same speed; other times it seems as if you are falling behind. Still, in rare instances you may feel you are ahead of the curve, kicking time's ass. But don't get too cocky; this is an illusion, for you are only as good as your last expedited, shipped and delivered package.

Two steps forward and one step back.

THE PAST IS HISTORY AND THE FUTURE IS A MYSTERY

74

Just as mystics and philosophers since the dawn of writing, drawing, sculpting, recording and publishing have suggested, we can only experience the 'now'. If you consider whatever happened to you in the past can no longer exist (except for in your memory), nor can you currently experience anything you imagine about the future (except via your imagination), you may commune with the source from which everything originates.

 It is impossible to be anywhere but here and now.

75

MANAGE YOUR ENERGY

Another way of saying this is 'go with
the flow'. Depleting or draining your
energy to the point of no return is
a sure way to mismanage your time.
If you want to be effective, you
must account for your well-being and
conduct yourself in a manner that
will conserve and convey your stamina
and strength. Without emotional,
physical and spiritual reserves in
your hopper, you are near useless. And
when that happens, all time management
strategies go the way of the dodo.

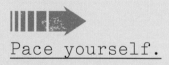

Pace yourself.

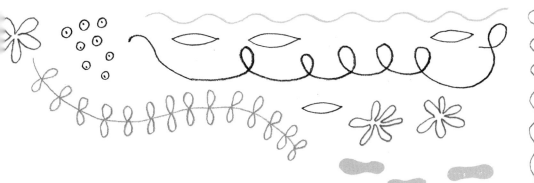

SCHEDULE CREATIVE TIME

76

Barring pharmaceutical and psychological cure-alls, creativity could be the answer to all your problems. Set aside seven minutes a day (the more the better) to play and explore and experiment and mess up. Give yourself the opportunity to play and you will be amazed. There are worlds unexplored inside you. All you need to do is give yourself the time to wander through the mist to uncover the original, colourful, innovative and/or visionary inclinations just waiting to burst out of you onto the page or screen or via a raw material.

Inside everyone is a child yearning to come out and play.

77

COOK IN BULK

Gather friends, family and neighbours together for a cooking or baking day. Better yet, convene at your local community kitchen or in the basement of your church and cook up a storm. On the other hand, if you prefer your own company, simply purchase all the storage containers and ingredients you need and whip up a week's worth of meals, snacks or treats. Instead of baking one batch of brownies, bake five. Then freeze them for a rainy day and/or take them to work for some 'brownie points'.

Fill your freezer with frozen pies, lasagnes, pierogies, soup, pizza dough, chilli, cookies or homemade loaves of bread.

78

PERSONALISE YOUR NEWS

Inundated with doom and gloom? Bombarded with facts and figures that mean little to you? Get only the information you need, when you need it, and you will free up cumulative years of your life. Do you love sports? Subscribe and only tune into your favourite sports news channels, blogs or shows. If you are interested in the latest scandal or conspiracy, set alerts for key words that satisfy your insatiable appetite for this salacious gossip. Limiting your exposure to the sources of information you find the most relevant will empower you to ignore the rest.

No need to suffer through the onslaught just so you can participate in shallow party conversation.

DON'T CHECK YOUR LUGGAGE

You can easily shave off an afternoon and otherwise spend it by the pool with a cocktail in hand by travelling light and carrying everything (in authorised containers) with you in your carry-on luggage when boarding a plane, boat, bus or train. Otherwise, you may never see your Bermuda shorts, Hard Rock Café tank-top or near-indistinguishable knock-off accessory from your exotic holiday again. That is the worst case scenario. On a good day, you will still stand around watching the clock tick slowly by while waiting for your belongings to arrive at baggage reclaim.

No need to prove that patience is a virtue.

80

LEARN TO SPEED READ

Only for the truly time-conscious, speed reading is an advanced personal and professional development strategy for only the keenest of learners.

If your reading comprehension skills are well-developed, why not see how much you can cram into your brain? Resources are numerous and abundant if you are serious about filling your knowledge base to the brim. Heck, why not go for a world record?

If you love to read, but don't have the time, speed reading could be the answer to your literary prayers.

DIGITISE YOUR MEMORABILIA

Is your garage, basement or attic filled to the brim with old scrapbooks, photo albums, crafts, folk art and music or movie collections? Do you rent a storage locker to deal with the overflow? If the answer to either of these questions is yes, it's time to scan, digitally photograph, and 'burn' all your memorabilia onto physical hard drives, so you may reduce the amount of clutter cluttering up your living space. If you are not technically savvy, bribe or employ a keen youngster to help you out. They could even send it up to heaven (the cloud) for safekeeping.

<u>Digital files don't deteriorate or take up space.</u>

82 USE GPS

How did you ever manage without it? But you did. And now you don't have to. The global positioning system has your back, literally, and as you probably know, can pinpoint your location anywhere on the planet within a few metres. Scary? Yes. Essential? Probably not. Helpful? Absolutely. So you never need lose time by getting lost again. Forewarned is forearmed.

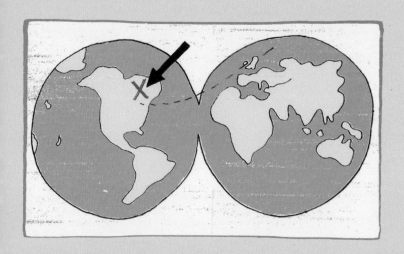

If you spend a lot of time behind the wheel, opt for the hands-free, voice-controlled model.

83

COMMUNICATE

When you are planning your day, week, month
or year, consult with and communicate with
whomever is involved. Few people are mind
readers, and you can't do much of anything
worthwhile alone, so you must communicate
your plans, wishes and feelings to the
people around you if you want to get
anything done in a timely manner. But this
is obvious. Where communicating becomes
more difficult is when you must share
what is in your heart, a timepiece unlike
any other. Would you agree that sensitive
matters require more attention and care
than sharing your mundane timetable?

Speaking from your heart
is never a waste of time.

SHOP ONLINE

Most online retailers wisely offer free shipping and no-hassle return and refund policies because they know many people prefer to physically examine a product before they purchase it. Often faster, easier and less expensive than shopping on Oxford Street, the benefits of online shopping are obvious. Ever-increasing competition on the Internet forces retailers of every shape and size — who offer anything your heart desires — to continuously innovate, which means more options and greater savings for you.

Keep your credit card frozen in a block of ice, because the world is at your fingertips.

85

LET YOUR FINGERS DO THE WALKING

The largest telephone directory
publisher in North America rode on
the coattails of this simple motto
for decades. Whether their in-house
marketing department or outside ad
agency hatched this golden egg matters
little; what does matter is that the
essence of time management had been
encapsulated in six simple words that
would educate the masses on the benefits
of flipping through their phone books
instead of wasting time.

Use your digits,
not your feet.

86

BUY IN BULK

The more you buy in bulk quantities, the less you have to go shopping. And the less you have to shop, the less you will get stuck in traffic, the less you have to queue and waste time searching for the goods you wish to consume. If this concept appeals to you, know that you are not alone; bulk stores exist for a reason, nor will you be labelled as a hoarder, unless you have already begun stockpiling for the zombie apocalypse (in which case you already know the benefits of buying in bulk).

To save even more time and money, organise a bulk-purchasing group in your neighbourhood, community or within your extended family.

87

HELP FROM YOUR FRIENDS

When you need some help, instead of begging for assistance or offering bribes, appeal to your helper's self-interest and they will be crewing your ship before you grant them permission-to-board. Save yourself the headache of headhunting by asking nicely and explaining why your helper is the right person for the job. Do this and you will have fewer crew members jumping ship or walking the plank at the end of your broad sword.

Many hands make for less work.

'Do you remember what a great job you did putting up that wallpaper at Tony's house last year? I was just wondering if I could ask you some questions.'

'Honey, I need a few things from the supermarket. Could you run down there for me? You can spend whatever is left over on a treat for yourself and your sister.'

'How about we do this together? You work on it today and I will finish it tomorrow.'

'I would be happy to write a review for your business if you would agree to help out with the fundraiser next month.'

'Would you like to come over for dinner this weekend? I loved that dessert you made last time — it was divine.'

'Hi Barb. Something has come up. Can I drop Billy off at your house this afternoon for an hour while I run some errands? I would be happy to return the favour next week.'

FILL UP YOUR PETROL TANK

You may see running out of petrol as an adventure in rare instances, but drifting to a complete stop on the motorway (or anywhere unplanned) is no fun. Nor is constantly pit-stopping for £10 of petrol here-and-there or even coasting into town on fumes. When you are at the petrol station, top the car up. Or better yet, get the nanny, spouse or kids to do it.

88

A more fuel-efficient vehicle will pay for itself in time and money saved.

89

ASK FOR THE BILL IN ADVANCE

Trim at least a few minutes off every night out by requesting that your waiter square up with you soon after finishing your meal (that is unless you left your wristwatch at home and have no intention of going back for it). In a busy restaurant, especially when you are in a hurry, expediting this often lengthy process can easily get you out the door and on your way lickety-split.

Reserve this tip for only when you truly need to hightail it out of there.

90

TURN OFF YOUR PHONE

When was the last time you turned your phone off? Yes, they are absolute marvels of technological progress, near-genius machines that have made our lives enormously productive and efficient, but they could also be robbing you of time better spent. Not only communication devices, smart phones are now capable of super-human feats, which, if utilised, put you at a distinct advantage. But be honest: How much of your screen time are you devoting to exploiting these advantages?

➡️

Press the off button
and put your phone
down for one day.

GET OFF THE GRID

Seemingly endless demands on your time wash it all down the drain, never to be seen or heard from again. Time speeds up the busier you are, because you are surrounded with distractions, responsibilities, decisions and hordes of demands on your resources. But all is not lost. You can slow to a standstill and still survive. The secret is to retreat from all the hustle and bustle. Do this and you may feel like you are holding time in your hand.

Step off the carousel and bend the space-time continuum once in a while.

92

LEARN TO TYPE FASTER

How many words per minute can you accurately type? Like many people, you likely don't handwrite and address letters one-at-a-time, so how long does it take you to compose an email? Not that typing is a race; but being able to effectively communicate with a keyboard can speed up your distant correspondence when the phone is not an option. If you already use all your fingers and thumbs to type, congratulations. Now take an online test to see where you can improve.

If you currently type with only two fingers, just imagine what you could do with 10.

93

THE PERFECT TEMPERATURE

A minor fix, but a fix
nonetheless, setting your
thermostat to match your habits,
schedule and routine will not
only save you messing with it on a
daily basis, but also save time by
keeping you from picking a sweater
from your closet, taking it on
and off, opening and shutting
windows and blinds and chopping,
splitting and stacking wood for
your fireplace.

Programming your
thermostat will teach
you (or force you) to
schedule your day.

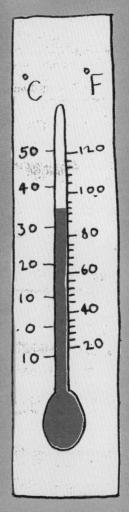

94

EAT BETTER

If you want more time to experience
the ups and downs of life, make
better choices. Food is both fuel and
medicine, so the higher the quality
of fuel and medicine you put into
your body, the healthier you will be.
And the healthier you are, the longer
you will live. Typical supermarkets
are filled with 40,000 chemically
engineered and preservative-laden
foods that will tend to shorten your
time here on earth, should you choose
to ingest them. Now if you desire to
change your diet, but don't know where
to start, visit a nutritionist.

Begin by eating unprocessed,
natural 'whole' foods.

95

BECOME A BETTER LISTENER

Everyone wants to be heard. And everyone wants to feel like their opinions, thoughts and feelings are valued. Once you become a better listener, you will find that opportunities jump into your lap. Important people will be more willing to trust you and you will find that your relationships are stronger and more satisfying. You have nothing to lose, except the time you previously squandered by not listening in the first place, and having to be reminded of instructions you were given, important details you ignored or sensitive information you were entrusted with.

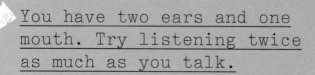

You have two ears and one mouth. Try listening twice as much as you talk.

96 SAVE MORE MONEY

If time is money, then saving more money will free up more time. More money in the bank will increase your self-esteem. More money in your pocket will allow you to make healthier choices at the supermarket. And more money invested will bring you inner peace by knowing that one day you will be able to retire and enjoy the fruits of your labour. Like bankers, credit counsellors, economists and advisors have professed for decades, saving at least some of your hard-earned money is prudent financial planning which will deduct years of slavery working at a job you may not love.

Sound financial literacy begins with saving 10% of everything you earn.

97 TURN OFF THE TV

Turning on the TV has become a habit. We all switch on the TV to relax and unwind at the end of the day. But is it making you happier? TV watching can actually make you feel unhappy and unmotivated. The lack of movement is not good for body or mind. Not too long ago, we didn't have an endless selection of channels and programmes. Adding more choices often only adds more stress, because the number of unwatched shows piles up. And it's a huge time suck. The average American watches five hours of TV a day. If you've ever wished for a few more hours in your day, this is the answer. Make a conscious decision to tune in to a limited number of shows you really want to watch — and then turn the TV off when they're over.

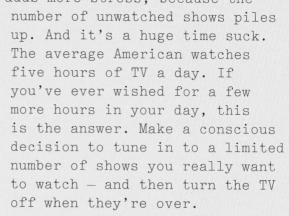

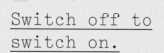

Switch off to switch on.

98

INCREASE YOUR MORTGAGE PAYMENT FREQUENCY

Shorten your commitment to your pledge of time and money to the lenders by making bi-weekly (or weekly) payments vs shelling out your funds on a monthly basis. Depending on how much and when interest charges are levied, you could save yourself thousands (which, apart from being more money in your pocket, can quickly free up time you would otherwise spend working to pay for the roof over your head).

 Make an appointment with your banker or mortgage broker as soon as possible.

99 AVOID PEAK TRAVEL TIME

This is a no-brainer, but most of us end up waiting in line, cursing the people in front of us and the service at the counter/booth/gate ahead of us. Yes, we are often confined to travelling at peak times because our schedules coincide with everyone else's. But there is a price to pay for freedom. Maybe take Friday off. Or, if everyone is taking Friday off, take Thursday off. Or camp in the backyard. Or get the relatives to visit you for a change. At peak times, everyone on the road or at the airport or on public transport is usually on edge, so 'getting there is half the fun' loses its sparkle when braving the hustle and bustle of bottle-neck transportation hubs.

 Nothing is as draining as waiting in line and watching time tick by.

Take Friday off. Or, if everyone is taking Friday off,
take Thursday off. Or camp in the backyard. Or get the
relatives to visit you for a change.

At peak times, everyone is usually on edge, so 'getting
there is half the fun' loses its sparkle when braving
the hustle and bustle of bottle-neck transport hubs.

Avoid rush hour (if at all possible) so you can spend
more time doing what you love, with the people you love.
Instead of waiting in line.